IMAGES OF ENGLAND

AROUND
NORTON

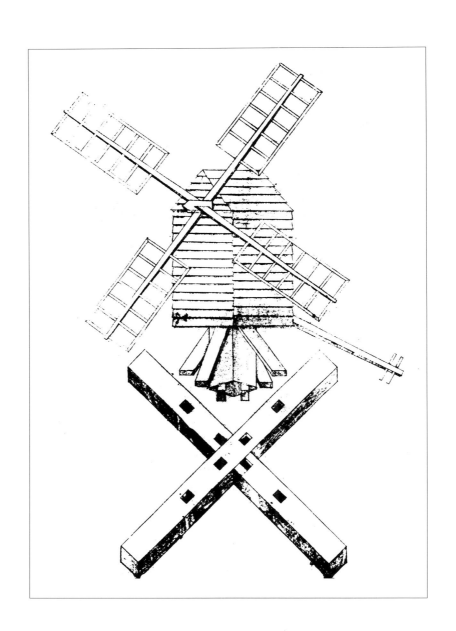

IMAGES OF ENGLAND

AROUND
NORTON

NORTON HISTORY GROUP

TEMPUS

Frontispiece: In the time of Queen Elizabeth I, this small post-mill stood on the hilltop at Herdings, then the home of yeoman farmer Jerome Rawlinson or Rollinson, and it was visible for miles around. The sketch plan was included in the record of proceedings of a lawsuit surrounding the corn mill in 1596. Such mills took their names from the construction method, with slots in the base to support posts on a 'leg'. Another corn mill driven by wind is recorded at the nearby hilltop at Coal Aston.

First published 2005

Tempus Publishing Limited
The Mill, Brimscombe Port,
Stroud, Gloucestershire, GL5 2QG
www.tempus-publishing.com

British Library Cataloguing in Publication Data.
A catalogue record for this book is available from the British Library.

ISBN 0 7524 3656 2

Typesetting and origination by Tempus Publishing Limited.
Printed in Great Britain.

Contents

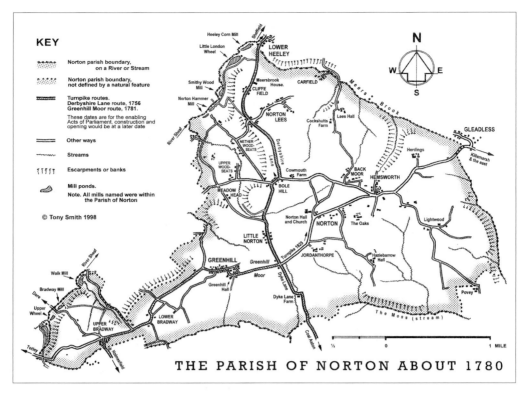

THE PARISH OF NORTON ABOUT 1780

This map shows the extent of the old parish of Norton before it was carved up into today's smaller ecclesiastical parishes and clearly indicates the scattered settlements and the two turnpike routes. Much of the area was farmed, although there is evidence of corn, paper and cutlers' mills on the banks of the River Sheaf. The rural hamlets of Upper and Nether Woodseats would be a great contrast to the now busy A61 Chesterfield Road. On the north-eastern edge, the Meers Brook not only separated Yorkshire and Derbyshire but also the provinces of York and Canterbury and, in earlier times, Northumbria and Mercia.

Introduction

The Norton History Group was founded in 1989 by the late Bernard Cooper to provide a forum for a group of people interested in researching and recording the history of the Parish of Norton. As well as searching archives, preserving records and collecting the photographs which form the basis of this book and its popular predecessor (*Norton*, published by Tempus in 2000), it was felt to be important to encourage older members of the community to record for posterity their memories of bygone days. The gift of photographs and information for captions were the result of conversations between Group members and long-standing residents.

A common theme was how much had altered in the last two or three generations. The pace of change does seem to be accelerating but there never was a golden age when life remained unaltered from generation to generation. Imagine the effect in the late sixteenth century when the local scythe- and sickle-making industries were given a boost of manpower and expertise by a group of immigrant Flemings. They had suffered persecution in the Netherlands and had been encouraged by the Earl of Shrewsbury to settle in Norton and Eckington.

When the *Sheffield Daily Telegraph* was lamenting the loss of a farm in Little Norton Lane in 1937, it said, 'The rural isolation of this delightful district is disappearing before the encroaching "modern residences". At one time – not so many years ago – a visit to Sheffield was quite an event for the people of Norton and the outlying areas beyond.' The photographs in this volume illustrate both the rapid changes that have taken place over the last century and also the continuity of life in Norton. This continuity has been emphasised by those whose memories reach back for almost three generations.

One of the most significant collections of photographs came from Edward Jessop, the Group's founder President, who died in 1998. Ted started work as a butcher's boy in Woodseats in the early 1920s and delivered to the large houses in Norton. He built up an encyclopaedic knowledge of the history of the area from the occupants, especially Mrs Bagshawe at The Oakes and the Revd Walker Hall at the Rectory and had vivid recollections of that time. As a teenager he had purchased a copy of *Chantreyland* and was so impressed that he wrote to Harold Armitage expressing his appreciation. So began a lifelong friendship, both men sharing a common love of the old rural Norton.

Armitage had anticipated the rapid expansion of Sheffield to almost engulf the ancient village but, as illustrated here, there are still parts of Norton which he would recognise instantly. Perhaps the biggest change has been in the way of life of its inhabitants. On Christmas Eve 1912, the Revd Walker Hall wrote to his aunt, 'Your grandchildren certainly help you to keep up Christmas in the old lively way – I expect to have some lively young people about me tomorrow in the shape of about twenty Choir-boys – They come to have their Christmas dinner at the Vicarage before they go out carolling which occupies the rest of the day. But it is not all carolling, I am told, as they get a good many mince-pies and other sweet-meats etc. at the different houses which they go to.' Times have changed indeed.

If this book enables people to remember those things which have been lost, encourages them to be vigilant both in preserving and finding new uses for our remaining old buildings and guarding our much needed open spaces, then it will have served as an appropriate memorial to all those whose recollections have helped to produce it.

Acknowledgements

We extend our grateful thanks to the many people who have given or lent us photographs, some of which were the treasured possessions of older family members and friends. Other people have given permission for us to use copyright material and have supplied us with information for the captions. We hope that the following list does not omit any names, but if your name is not included please accept our apologies. Some names are of people who have died recently but whose contributions we wish to acknowledge.

John Eaton Trustees; the Head of Leisure Services, Sheffield City Council for permission to use two photographs; the staff of the Local Studies Library and of Sheffield Archives, the Libraries, Archives and Information Department, for their unfailing help; Heritage House Group Ltd; Norton Free School; Norton Oakes Cricket Club; Norton Ploughing Association; Sheffield Local Education Authority; Sheffield Newspapers Ltd. Local photographers we have been unable to trace: C.H. Lea, Noel, L.D. Swift.

V. Aitchison, E. Archer, M. Asby, F.M. Atterwill, A. Bocking, J. Bower, A. Brackenbury, J. Brackenbury, G.D. Brooks, S. Burrows, J. Carr, R. Constantine, V. Curley, M. Dean, I. Denton, J. Elliott, S. Elliott, R. Flint, D. Foster, F.N. Gibbs, A. Gilmour, P. Haddock, B. Hanwell, T. Hanwell, F. Harrison, J. Hawley, R. Heppenstall, D. Higgins, M. Hughes, P.C. Hyde-Thomson, E. Jessop, H. Jones, I. Koszalinski, R. Lee, B. Maynard, D. Memmott, R. Nicholls, R. Padley, N. Parker, J. Parkin, G. Platts, E. Powell, L. Price, R. Randall, C. Richards, J. Robinson, C. Rodgers, W. Ryals, A.R. Shaw, D. Shepherd, A.V. Smith, P. Snape, R. Stevens, B. Stones, B. Symonds, M. Thomas, W.A. Timperley, S. Tongue, R. Unwin, S. Vardy, K. Warrington, J. White, W. Wildgoose, M. Williams, D. Williamson, R. Wilson, R. Wollaston, O. Young.

Members of Norton History Group who lent photographs and who worked on the book include: Michael Bland, Pamela Bower, Maureen Fleming, Sheila Gilmour, Alan Hill, Joy Phillips, Anne Phipps, Kathryn Simpson, Margaret Vardy and Margaret Wilmott.

one

The Oakes-
in-Norton

The Oakes-in-Norton in the 1930s was owned by the Isherwood-Bagshawe family. Norton's famous sculptor, Sir Francis Chantrey, designed both the terrace and the urns. Sir William Bagshawe remodelled the house in a Georgian, neo-classical style between 1811 and 1827. The last members of the Bagshawe family to live at the Oakes moved out to Wormhill in 1984, two years after the opening of Bochum Parkway.

The eastern gates to the Oakes have a central medallion with the initials R.B. for Richard Bagshawe, who occupied the Oakes in the early eighteenth century. These gates had been missing for many years but were recently discovered on the estate, although in a poor state of repair.

Right and below: This ornamental gate, long gone, was in the north wall of the vegetable and fruit garden at the Oakes. On the far side of the high wall at the south end is a range of greenhouses and a potting shed. The garden was not oblong, but widened to the south; thus the wall on the eastern boundary had a south-westerly aspect, favourable for growing peaches and nectarines. Protection from frost was ensured by building a thick, double wall through which flues ran, heated by fires in furnaces built into the wall.

Miss Beatrice Muriel Bagshawe in 1907 in her wedding dress, thought to have been made in Paris. She generously donated a five-panelled altar frontal to St James's Church, made from material used for her wedding dress. Villagers erected magnificent decorative arches to greet her and her husband on their return from honeymoon.

Right: Mr and Mrs Henry Bradshaw Isherwood-Bagshawe lived at the Oakes after their marriage. The bride's surname, Bagshawe, was added to that of her husband, in order to keep the historic connection between the Bagshawe family and the Oakes estate. Mrs Isherwood-Bagshawe was presented at court in 1908.

Below: Mr Kimber, the estate manager at the Oakes, accompanying Mrs Muriel Isherwood-Bagshawe, centre, and her younger sister, Miss Gladys Bagshawe. The ladies were mounted side-saddle in the fashion of the time and often made use of the several mounting blocks situated around the village.

The coat-of-arms over the stable window at the Oakes shows quarters of the Bagshawe, Gill, Westby and Drake families. The motto translates as 'Beauty is the glory; fame is empty'.

The oak panelling surrounding the drawing-room fireplace is in the style of Inigo Jones and may be either late seventeenth or early eighteenth century. The walls of the room were at one time hung with family portraits of the Gill and Drake families. There was also a portrait of Charles II as a child.

Summoned by bells! The plaques under each bell indicated the name or number of the room which the Bagshawe family servants were called to attend. These bells were located downstairs near the kitchen.

The organ was built in London in 1792 for William Chambers Bagshawe, who was a talented musician, mastering six instruments. It was moved to the alcove in the dining room around 1837, when the music room upstairs was turned back into a bedroom. The organ was sold in 1984 for £20,900 by Sotheby's and is now believed to be in Canada. The tapestries were brought to the Oakes from rooms in Sheffield Castle around 1646 and the statues are by Sir Francis Chantrey.

Above: The gardens at the Oakes are listed in the National Register of Parks and Gardens of Special Historic Interest and include this canal pond, known to be extant in 1753, and the daffodil walk beside it.

Left: The pigeon cote in the stable yard is a listed building, probably eighteenth century. Note the flight shelf on all sides. The square lantern with ogee dome shown here was damaged during a severe storm; the present lantern is a replacement.

Opposite, below: The date over the main door of the stables is 1722. Conversion to private dwellings was begun after the sale of Oakes-in-Norton in 1984. The main house was eventually bought by the Oakes Trust and, after extensive renovation, was opened as a Christian Youth Holiday Centre in 2000. Sympathetic renovation work continues to the house and grounds.

The view from the pigeon cote towards the east shows the rear of the stables and a well-kept wagon. In 1964 this still carried the name and address of Francis Westby Bagshawe, The Oakes-in-Norton, even though he had died in 1896! After the death of Mrs Isherwood-Bagshawe, the wagon and two horse-drawn coaches emblazoned with the family coat-of-arms were sold by Major T. Bagshawe.

Above: Feeding the bull in the stables at the Oakes in 1953 are Walter Timperley, George Billam and Harry Anderson.

Left: Wilfred Ryals, Evelyn Ryals and Harry Anderson at a Meet of the Barlow Hunt at the Oakes, *c.* 1950.

NORTON
AGRICULTURAL SHOW
Monday, Aug. 7th, 1950

Reserve

Class....*53*....   Exhibit No.....*49*....

Exhibitor...*R. Fox*...   Judge...*W. B. Wood*...

Wood, Printer, Penistone.

Major and Mrs T. Bagshawe were generous in allowing use of the grounds around the Oakes and the Norton Show was held there for many years. At one time the Norton Show included a wide range of competitive classes for animals, giving both farmers and youngsters a chance to win a prize. It is now held at Hazelbarrow Farm, on land near the Bochum Parkway.

Major Thornber and Mrs Hilary Bagshawe at the Oakes in the late 1980s, with the Revd Mark Williams of St James's, Norton. It became a custom during his time as rector to celebrate the Patronal Festival for St James with an old-fashioned picnic in the extensive grounds of the Oakes. Parishioners also enjoyed a game of rounders and strolling round the gardens.

It is believed that the ornamental wrought-iron gates at the Oakes-in-Norton were made of iron from the estate. The Lodge was built in the early nineteenth century with some twentieth-century additions.

May and Harry Anderson with Edna and George Billam enjoying 'a bit of a do' on the terrace at the Oakes. Both men worked on the estate, living nearby in School Lane and in Mawfa Lane.

The north side of Norton Green, School Lane, shortly before its demolition in 1974. The site can be pinpointed by locating the lime tree, which still stands at the corner of Cypress Avenue and School Lane.

The south side of Norton Green in 1973 with Mr Wilson, the last occupant, standing on the left talking to Harry Anderson. The house was rebuilt in this style in 1866 on the site of the much older Bowling Green House.

Above: Norton Green Lodge was built in the same style as the main house. It was demolished in 1956, to be replaced by a large bungalow with white walls and a green tiled roof. This, in turn, was demolished in the late 1960s.

Left: The Robinson family of Norton Green Lodge walking down to Hazelbarrow around 1941. Mr Robinson was a local ARP warden and always carried the box containing his gas mask. John attended Norton Free School and has happy memories of his time there.

Opposite, below: Norton Lane during the heavy snowfalls of 1947, taken from the bend by the Oakes Lodge, looking west. The ball finials of Norton Green Lodge gateposts can be made out, as well as Spring House and its outbuildings. Spring House was the village store and tea-room and at this date it was also the post office.

The rural nature of Norton Lane in the 1950s, looking towards the Oakes Lodge and Norton Green Lodge, centre right. The lane giving access to the cottages at Maugerhay is on the far right and the hedge boundary of Norton Free School playing fields is on the left.

Left: Norton Lane, looking towards the Chantrey Memorial obelisk (not visible), Norton House stables, the cruck barn and the wall to Norton House garden. In the late 1930s horses were kept in the stables and Miss Betty Wardle ran a riding school there.

Below: Norton House cruck barn in December 1959, shortly before its demolition. Norton Lane was then widened considerably. Seven houses were built on the site of the barn, stables and kitchen garden in 1967.

The inner yard of Norton House stables and cruck barn in December 1959. The buildings are drawn on a map of 1737 in exactly the same form. There was also a cottage to the left, as part of the stables complex. The tall, central archway led on to Norton Lane.

The Norton House cruck barn during its demolition in 1961. The barn, which had four or five bays, probably dated from the early 1600s, which was the date of the first Norton House on this site. The ridge tree or main beam of the roof was set diagonally between the square-cut ends of the cruck blades.

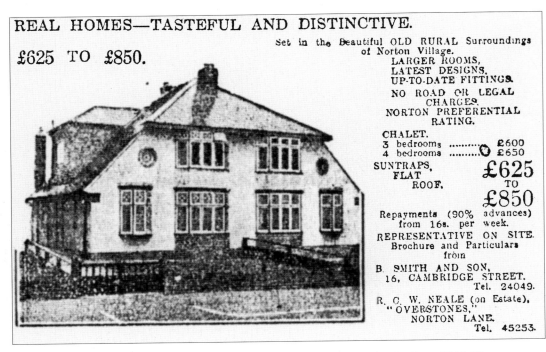

REAL HOMES—TASTEFUL AND DISTINCTIVE.

£625 TO £850.

Set in the Beautiful OLD RURAL Surroundings of Norton Village.
LARGER ROOMS,
LATEST DESIGNS,
UP-TO-DATE FITTINGS.
NO ROAD OR LEGAL CHARGES.
NORTON PREFERENTIAL RATING.

CHALET.
3 bedrooms £600
4 bedrooms £650

SUNTRAPS,
FLAT ROOF.

£625 TO £850

Repayments (90% advances) from 16s. per week.
REPRESENTATIVE ON SITE.
Brochure and Particulars from

B. SMITH AND SON,
16, CAMBRIDGE STREET.
Tel. 24049.

R. C. W. NEALE (on Estate),
"OVERSTONES,"
NORTON LANE.
Tel. 45253.

The houses advertised here in 1937 were built on the Norton House estate by the firm of M.J. Gleeson, starting in 1934. Variations of this design can be seen in the area today.

The Norton House estate looking north up Cloonmore Drive from Henley Avenue in the 1930s. This shows both the 'chalet bungalow' and 'sun trap' flat-roofed style of house.

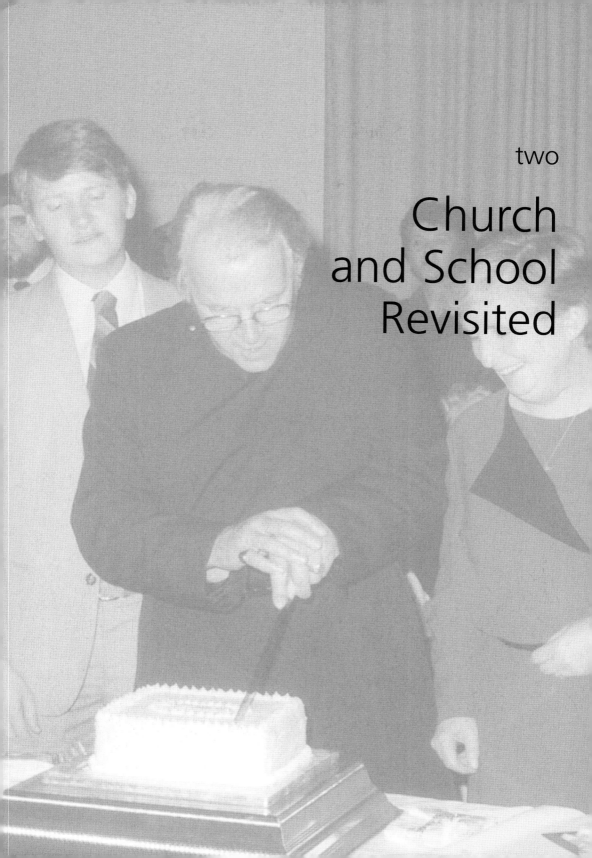

two

Church
and School
Revisited

The Church Hall at Norton was opened in June 1951, the first of three proposed centres within the parish to be completed. An appeal fund had been launched in 1947, to which the parish contributed nearly £4,000. The Bishop of Derby's Ten-Year Plan added a further £3,000. The hall, built of rustic brick on a pre-cast concrete frame, was finished inside in green and cream and included a stage, retiring rooms and an 'easy-clean' kitchen.

Youth Club members, including Mollie Wilson, Malcolm Coombs, Rosemary Gledhill, Madelaine Baine, Michael Hodinott and Malcolm Stubbs in the Vicarage Field in the late 1940s. Mr Shepherd, a local farmer, cut the hay and cared for the field in general.

The Revd Mark Williams, Rector of St James's from 1974-1989, celebrated the twenty-fifth anniversary of his priesting in September 1985. During a special service taken by the Bishop of Sheffield, the churchwardens presented the rector with a white stole to mark the occasion. A buffet followed in the Church Hall for friends and parishioners. The Revd Williams was joined in the cake-cutting by his wife Enfys and their children Paul, Katie and Jonathan.

Preparing for a Scout jumble sale on 17 March 1990. The Youth Hall on the right was the meeting place for the Scout and Guide groups. The twice-yearly jumble and furniture sales have long been a recognised part of Norton life and customers often travelled from a wide area to wait for bargains, forming long queues up to an hour before opening.

In this view of St James's, a small white area can be seen on the wall of the Garden of Remembrance. This was a mosaic, designed by Mr Ron Padley, using Epstein's figure of Christ for his inspiration. The mosaic was constructed in the Padley's spare bedroom from one-inch square tiles stuck onto a brown paper backing. It was tricky, heavy work moving it along to the churchyard. It was very disappointing when a tree blew down in the great gale of 1962, smashing part of the wall and shattering the mosaic beyond repair.

Above: Henry Harrison & Sons, the well-known firm of masons and builders, was established in 1885. At one time they were based at 52 Little Norton Lane but are now in Greenfield Road. Here five men are at work on the roof of St James's Church, Norton, in 1928/9. Jim Harrison, son of Henry, is wearing the bowler hat.

Right: Remains of an old archway are clearly visible in the north aisle of St James's. The galleries in the church were cramped and low-ceilinged so in 1820 one pillar was removed from each side of the nave, thus allowing the three-decker pulpit to be seen. These two pillars were replaced during the 1881/2 restoration by George Edmund Street.

The remains of an old Elizabethan window in the western churchyard wall, marking the boundary between the church and Norton Hall. It may have been part of a much earlier hall on the site. The ground level is much raised now, being almost on a level with the sill.

Norton Hall Lodge at the Norton Church Road entrance to the Hall, in the 1930s. Originally one of three entrance lodges to the estate, it was renovated in 1998 and is now a private residence. St James's Church is visible on the left and part of the roof of Norton Hall can be seen in the background to the right. The ball finial on the gatepost is no longer in place.

By 1993 the buildings round the stable yard at Norton Hall had become dilapidated. A haulage firm had used the barn on the right until the farm buildings, far right, were converted into houses. The small door near the front led into very large stalls where shire horses had been stabled and where, for a while, the Scout Group stored waste paper that they had collected locally.

During the conversion to apartments, the builders found many traces of H.M. Forces based at the yard in both world wars. Among the cigarette packets, playing cards and a laundry list was a poster for a Cruiser Week in March 1918. We hope that people believed that 'Your money will be quite safe!' and saved enough for three new cruisers, as requested.

Gleadless Valley School opened in September 1961 under the headship of Mr G.M. Hughes. It was a very successful school with a variety of activities and modern facilities such as this domestic science kitchen. By 1993, although now a comprehensive school, numbers had been reduced from 900 to 500 pupils. It was thought to be too small and so was closed.

The staff at Gleadless Valley School in 1979. From left to right, front row: S. Foster, N. Jepson, C. Richards, D. Bradley, G. Howe, F. Cooper, H. Lamb, F. Johnson, R. Dunn, D. Roden, M. Broadhurst, B. Kentzer, D. Cross. Second row: Mrs Saville, M. Timms, M. Francis, -?-, G. Mathieson, K. Meakin, O. Young, L. Hudson, M. McDermott, B. Chapman, M. Russell, -?-, J. Ledger, -?-, -?-, B. Muggeridge. Third row: M. Pierce, P. Whitehead, R. Lyons, G. Saville, P. Martin, J. Hull, J. Morgan, A. Green, H. Pashley, G. Barnaby, S. Wilson, H. Lamb, J. Kershaw. Back row: J. Francis, -?-, B. Wainwright, K. Simpson, B. Proctor, T. Sewell, C. Smith, M. Didier, B. Moffat, M. Heald, T. Pashley.

Class 2 at Norton Free School in 1907 with Mr Atkin, Headmaster. Children with well-known Norton surnames, including Biggin, Billam, Binney, Birtles, Cuzner, Earnshaw, Knowles, Lee, Rhodes and Spittlehouse, were attending the school at this time.

PREVIOUS ATTENDANCE.

I certify that *Ewart Matthews*

residing at *36 Mount View Rd* .... SHEFFIELD,

has made 350 attendances in not more than two schools during each

year for five preceding years, whether consecutive or not, as shown

by the (1) certificate furnished by the Principal Teacher of the (2)

Sheffield *Park Grove* .... School.

(Signed) *.............................*

Secretary to the Sheffield Education Committee.

Dated the *21* day of *Sept.* 1911.

(1) For this Certificate see Schedule VI.
(2) Here name School or Schools in which the attendances have been made.

Part of a Labour Certificate which had to be filled in when a pupil became thirteen. Ewart Matthews was born on 1 August 1898 so by 21 September 1911 had reached the school leaving age. A few districts had raised the age to fourteen by this time. (The family now uses one t in the surname.)

Above: The retiring and new Norton Free School May Queens visiting the Jessop Hospital annexe, Norton Hall, in 1954. From left to right, Queens Julie Wallace and Jennifer Bedford; Attendants Ann Fowkes, Vickie Curley, Linda Hardwick and Pamela ?. The flower girls include Nina Latham on the far left; the remaining six names are not known.

Left: Mrs Bedford and Jennifer outside the Girls' Entrance to Norton Free School, *c.* 1949. The housing for the school bell is visible on the roof. The restored bell was rung by Bishop Jack Nichols of Sheffield at the official opening of the new school on 20 January 2004, almost 350 years after the school's foundation.

Norton Free School class of 1962. From left to right, back row: Mrs Walker, Simon Smith, Mark Smith, Rosemary Storey, Keith Walton, Ian Ringstead, Michael Dewar, Mr Walch. Middle row: Tina Hurt, Sheila Booth, Amanda Ellis, Anita Bocking, Gillian Wilkinson, Fay Bradbury, Stephen Bashforth, Byron Edley, Carol Wheelhouse. Front row: Stephen Lake, Timothy Stewart, Peter Sargenson, Elizabeth Rotchell, Adrian Smith, Richard Smith, Jane Parr, Jill Ashby, Peter Hughes, David Purcell, Martin Dooley.

Norton Free School Sports Day in 1964 was held on the running track and field where the new school building now stands. The flat-roofed 'Derwent-type' classrooms have been demolished and the area is now the staff car park. The old 1895 building remains, for the present in the ownership of the Diocese of Sheffield.

Norton Free School staff in September 1965. From left to right, back row: Mr R.J. Britton, Mrs V. Simpson, Mrs J.M. Mellors, Mr J. MacGregor. Front row: Mrs P.M. Housley, Headmaster Mr H. Walch, Mrs C.I. Walker.

A school visit in 1963, possibly to Coventry Cathedral. Staff members – wearing hats and gloves! – were, from left to right: Mrs Housley, Mrs Walch, Mrs Simpson.

The Junior playground in 1962, before the extra classrooms were added. The garage on the right was demolished and the outdoor toilets, seen on the left, were replaced during the extensions in 1963.

Children enjoying May Day revels in 1963 include Gillian Cundy, Rosemary Phillips, Andrew Rotchell, Judith Ashby, Elizabeth Hallett, Linda McCreery, Robert Holmes, Leonie Plumtree and Katherine Crawford. Behind them are the school fields, with a central hedge, and a glimpse of the bungalow on the site of the old Norton Green Lodge.

Above and below: Preparing the foundations of the new classrooms in 1963, linking the Oakes annexe, built in 1957, with the old school. The water tower, completed in 1961, is an important landmark in the south of Sheffield. It is worth visiting on the occasions when it is open to the public because a fine panorama can be viewed from the Observation Gallery.

Above and below: Mr H. Walch, Mr E. Crookes and pupils taking part in a practical maths lesson, using the completed foundations for the Derwent-type classrooms. The lower photograph shows the construction of walls as the classrooms take shape.

Victorian style re-enactment of a football match first played on 3 April 1890 when the score was Norton Free 5, Meersbrook Bank 0. The score in 1974 was Norton 4, Meersbrook 2. From left to right, back row: Junior 4 teacher Mr J. Driscoll, David Oldale, Graham Hall, Ernest Bool, John Bamford, John Harper, David Potts, Adrian Brammer. Middle row: Andrew Mullins, Stephen Gray, Shaun Day, Thomas Bell, Richard Dyson. Front row: David Morris, Andrew Fleming.

The Queen's Silver Jubilee in 1977 was celebrated in many ways at Norton Free School. Heavy rain on that day created streams of red, white and blue across the playground, coming from crêpe paper used to decorate the children's bicycles.

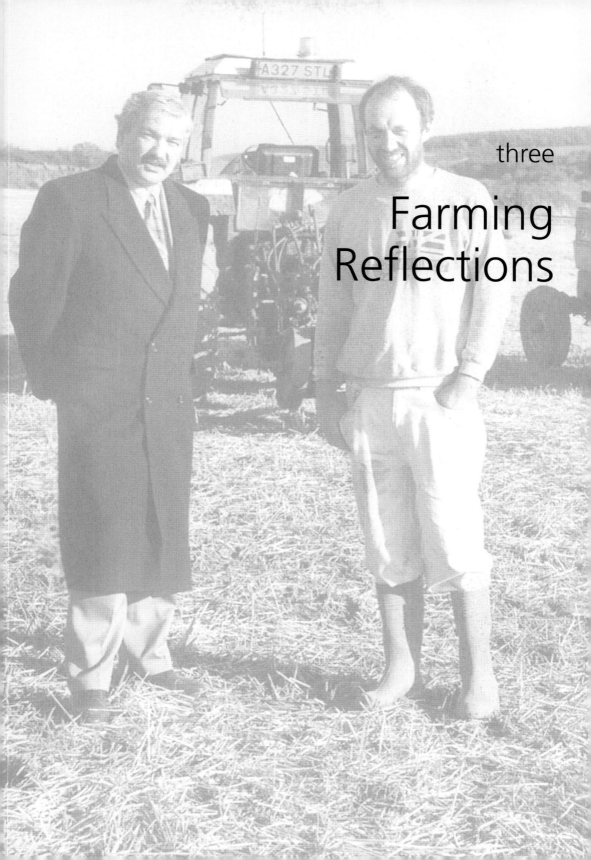

three

Farming
Reflections

The north elevation of Povey Farm in 1958 showing the seventeenth-century porch or entrance tower with its mullioned windows. The ancient farm was the property of Beauchief Abbey from at least the twelfth century and at one time was included with Haslehurst in one holding.

Gordon Thompson on horseback at the top of the yard at Povey in 1958, in front of the buildings which lie to the east of the farmhouse. Most farmers rode a horse around their farm and some have continued this practice to the present day. The barrels were full of whey, fed to the pigs together with whole milk to provide protein in their diet.

Stephen Thompson, the present farmer, talking to Alan Powell of *The Sheffield Telegraph* at the Norton Ploughing Association Match at Povey Farm in 1993. The Thompson family has farmed at Povey at the lower end of Lightwood Lane since the late nineteenth century.

Having a rest at the Norton Ploughing Association Match at Povey Farm in 1993. The gentleman on the right is Geoffrey Key from Hatton, near Derby.

Jimmy Walker (once of Grange Farm, Unstone), Charlie Rathbone, Pat Undrell and Ian Salter at the 1996 Ploughing Match. Paul Haddock is standing behind Mr Salter.

Derrick Marsden from Tickhill, with his horses Beauty and Gemma, closely watched by John King on his right, at the Norton Ploughing Association Match held at Povey in 1995. The horses on the far left, Beauty and Prince, belong to John Taylor of Ranskill.

The farmhouse at Lightwood, still often referred to as Spittlehouse's Farm, looked much the same in 1997 as it did in the eighteenth century. Two farms had the name Lightwood but recently this one has been renamed as Frogpool Farm.

The Lightwood Lane cottage and buildings on the left were referred to as the Dairy for many years. Mr Pocklington and his two sons had a poultry business and also ran a milk round from the house. Mr and Mrs Herbert Morton lived in the far cottage for a while; Mrs Morton sold home-made ginger-beer to thirsty hikers on their way down the valley.

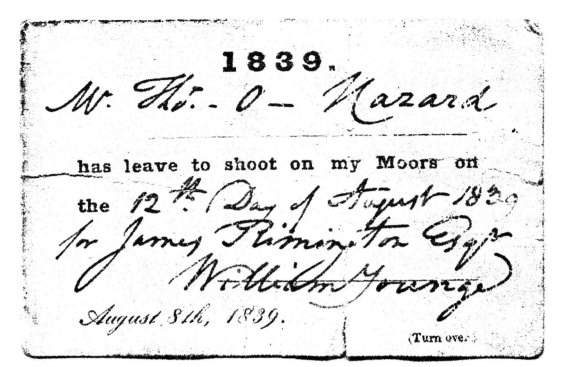

1839.

Mr. Tho. O. Hazard

has leave to shoot on my Moors on the 12th Day of August 1839 for James Rimington Esqr

William Younge

August 8th, 1839.

(Turn over.)

Above: Tommy Hazard of the Herdings was born and died in the old farm, which was saved from demolition in 1958. Several of his game certificates were found during renovations. This one had some conditions on the reverse side, including 'No shooting before 8 a.m.' and 'Ticket must be shown to any person authorized by me to require sight of it'.

Left: Two farms were at the Herdings, both of cruck construction. The western one, here seen from the east in 1949, was a dairy farm run by Mrs Shaw. After she was widowed, she married Percy Nutt. She and her sons delivered milk from a float pulled by a piebald horse. The farm was demolished in 1958 and three thirteen-storey point-blocks were built, two of which remain.

These white-washed cottages are shown on old maps, on the south side of Norton Avenue, downhill from the Herdings farms. The Hallam and Lee families are remembered living there between 1900 and 1910. The cottages were empty during the 1930s and were completely demolished in 1938 to make way for the No. 16 (Sheffield) Barrage Balloon Centre.

A plaque bearing the badge of the No. 3 Radio and Radar Servicing Squadron, Signals Command, which moved to the site of the No. 16 (Sheffield) Barrage Balloon Centre in July 1943. This area was between the Herdings farms and Lightwood. The motto *Arte et Animo* translates roughly as 'With skill and pride'.

Above: William Fielding was the landlord of the Bagshawe Arms until he bought Spring House in 1900. He played an important part in parish life as committee member, surveyor of roads and commons and land drainer. The outside steps to the courtroom can be seen in the yard behind the farm workers.

Left: The Petty Sessions Courtroom was over the stables at the back of the Bagshawe Arms. The 1859 date stone can still be seen on this gable-end. The initials F.W.B. stand for Francis Westby Bagshawe of the Oakes, a local magistrate for a number of years.

Opposite, below: Mr Fernridge was a member of the Norton Home Guard platoon which met at the Bagshawe Arms. Another group met at the Transport Ground at Meadowhead and Norton House was the main Norton base. The Government disbanded the Home Guard at the end of 1944.

POST CARD.

FOR INLAND POSTAGE ONLY, THIS SPACE MAY NOW BE USED FOR COMMUNICATION.

THE ADDRESS ONLY TO BE WRITTEN HERE.

HALFPENNY STAMP.

Norton Conservative Association.

PRESIDENT : E. DICKINSON, ESQ.

THE CHRISTMAS SMOKER will be held at the **BAGSHAWE ARMS, NORTON** on **THURSDAY Evening, December 29th, 1904,** at **8 o'clock.**

All Members and Friends cordially invited.

R. HOWROYD,

WITH THE SEASONS COMPLIMENTS.

Hon. Sec.

This Christmas Smoker was one of many dinners and club meetings held at the Bagshawe Arms. One definition of a Smoker is 'a concert at which smoking is permitted'.

---

15 Platoon, ''D'' Coy., 65th W.R. Batt., Home Guard.

The next Parade will be on January 9th, 1944, at Bagshawe Arms, at 09-45 Hrs.

Thereafter you will report on ~~Mondays~~ / Tuesdays only at { Bagshawe Arms / ~~Norton House~~ } until further notice.

Sunday parades weekly as usual at Bagshawe Arms.

V T Howl . Lt

I/C. 15 Platoon

Mary Ann (*née* Rose) Archer (1846-1925) was the second wife of Robert Archer. Her sons, standing from left to right, were Albert Rose Archer (1873-1956) and his brother, William Archer (1875-1949).

William Archer, seen outside his house at Mawfa Lane in the 1940s, with his daughter Gwen standing in the doorway. His business was Joiner, Wheelwright and General Smith and he, his sons Cyril and Leslie, together with skilled workmen, served Norton from birth to death – villagers remember both cribs and coffins!

George Burnell, his wife Dora *née* Bullifant and two of their sons are remembered as farmers at Hemsworth. The old farm was shown on the 1804 survey map by Fairbank and it is lucky that a photograph exists because, like most of Hemsworth, the farm was demolished to make way for a housing estate.

Harry Bullifant, brother of Dora Burnell, ran Lodge Farm. Once part of the rural hamlet of Hemsworth, it has been surrounded by a council estate since the 1960s but at least the farmhouse survives. Both Harry and Dora lived until fairly recently, both reaching a great age.

The ancient Grange Farm Grade II-listed buildings are greatly changed now. After it was sold in 1984, people stripped the stone roof-slates and took stones away from the walls. The several cruck-bays were exposed and are too damaged to reclaim.

Wetlands is a name found in many old documents. The two cottages belonged to the Bagshawe family estate and at one time housed their gamekeeper in the left-hand cottage and their woodman on the right.

The local pig killer in 1953 was Mr Wilson, who lived in a cottage in Greenfield Road. The children (and a few adults) referred to him as Mr Pigsticker – but never to his face! This pig-block is still at Hazelbarrow Farm.

Hazelbarrow Farm Cottage when the ancient oak trees were still in the nearby hedgerow. Harold Armitage in *Chantreyland* mentions these and pictures a drawing of a fox on a weathervane. This was attached to the gable of the building beside the cottage.

An age-old scene of harvesting at Hazelbarrow. Six or eight sheaves were placed to make each stook, in readiness for taking to the stack-yard.

Ben Elliott pitching sheaves on to the wagon with his brother Douglas working on top. A tractor has replaced the use of a horse to pull the wagon.

four

Leisure and
Pleasure

Norton Oakes Cricket Club was formed in 1877 by Mr Bagshawe for servants and workers on his estate. Many Hemsworth and Backmoor families have memories of a father and grandfather who played in the early 1900s and who may be in this XI, playing a friendly match at Hartshead Friends' ground about 1905.

Norton Oakes Cricket Club First XI had a very successful season in 1948, winning the Cockayne Shield. From left to right, back row: T. Wildsmith, D. Coupe, E. Pocklington, J. Pearson, G. Beeson, E. Bagnall, C. Spittlehouse. Front row: I. Baxter, W. Cadman, R. Ford, R. Coupe, J.W. Allen, C. Holland.

Improvements were made to Norton Oakes cricket ground in 1953. New facilities for players and their families, seen here on a Match Day in 1960, included a changing hut, canteen and toilets.

Improvements continued to be made at Norton Oakes, everyone joining in the building of a new pavilion in 1964. Two sight-screens were purchased in 1969 and a groundsman's store, a score box and new changing rooms were added in 1976.

Girl Guides from St John's Church walking along Matthews Lane towards Graves Park on Whit Monday, *c.* 1964. Mrs Barbara Radford, their Guide Captain, is on the far left and the leading Guide is Janet Carr.

Members of St John's Church on the way back from the Whit Monday gathering in Graves Park, led by their Church Lads' Brigade band, *c.* 1964. The band includes Les Radford, the tall officer at the centre back, who was a lay reader at St John's, Alan Harris, the drummer on the right in the second row and Rod Dean, the drummer at the centre front.

Right: This alehouse is reputed to be the oldest in the area, dating from the early 1600s, when nail-making was a cottage industry. It was the right-hand cottage of a pair, both of which had ancient beams in the ceiling. Beer was drawn from a barrel in the cellar and brought in a large enamel jug through to a tiny front room, which had a stone floor, trestle tables and armchairs.

Below: Miners from Woodseats walked up to Hemsworth each morning to join friends from Norton, before continuing their journey to the various coal pits then operating to the south of Sheffield. William Birch Shaw, born in 1885, here sitting on the wall second from the left, worked at Birley from the age of twelve. Was it cold tea in the tin flasks?

Above and below: Members of the Denton family in the garden at Ashbury Drive in August 1947, including Mrs Exley, Mrs Denton senior, Mr Harry Denton, Mr Denton senior and Mrs Renée Denton. The view is from their garden looking east across the fields, long before the building of the Upper Gleadless Valley estate.

Right: Ron Lee in the garden of 5 Ashbury Lane in 1956. This group of mid-nineteenth century cottages once stood between the New Inn and the row of cottages still to be seen farther down the Lane. Mr Wheldon, the owner, numbered them from 1 to 5, forgetting the sixth one, entered from the back! Later, Sheffield Corporation added to the confusion, numbering them 7 to 11 and 15 to 19. Several of the families, e.g. Lee, Harrison, Rhodes, still live locally.

Below: The Lee boys of 5 Ashbury Lane visiting Dad in the park around 1943. From left to right: Derrick, Mr Lee, Mrs Lee, Ronald and Dennis.

Biggin and Lee families have lived in
Norton for at least 200 years. They are
remembered as file-cutters, shoemakers
and farmers. They also gave loyal service to
St James's Church. This is a family picture
of a Mrs Biggin, *née* Lee, who lived in
Blackmoor in the 1800s.

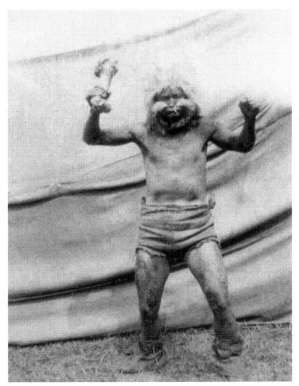

Leslie Powell and Walter Harrop arranged
a great double act for an August Bank
Holiday Gala, held in a field at Backmoor
in 1943. Mr Powell, in white plus-fours,
legs and arms adorned with red lipsticked
stars and moons, beat a gong and raised a
crowd. When enough had paid, the 'Wild
Man' appeared with a roar. Mr Harrop was
unrecognisable in his sugar-sack shorts and
boots, floor-mop hair and facial whiskers.
The two men raised £20 for the Red Cross.

Air-raid wardens, including Leslie Powell on the far right, at 9 Backmoor Road early in 1941. Mr Powell's son remembers bombs falling, one behind and one in front of the house. The family survived but damage to the roof and buildings was considerable. Stirrup pumps were used to fight small fires.

Members of the local ARP in 1941 at the Air Raid Precautions Post SB 5 and Emergency Room, situated at 9 Backmoor Road. They include C. Holland, Dr Timperley, A. Webb, L. Powell, Mrs Vardy, E. Day and Mrs Holland.

Left: John Eaton, born in Calais in 1832, was elected to Sheffield Town Council in 1873 and became the fifth lord mayor in 1900. His son, John Dickenson Eaton, left money to build almshouses named in memory of his father. The houses, intended for retired employees of the family chain of jewellery and pawnbroking businesses, are tucked away behind gardens on Hemsworth Road. This elegant shelter acts as a central meeting point of the paths in the extensive grounds.

Below: The John Eaton Almshouses were completed in 1941, consisting originally of twenty-eight single-storey houses, a reading room, a warden's house and a boardroom. At first the pensioners lived rent and rates free, with the services of a resident superintendent and matron. Residents still enjoy social events, including dances, whist drives, indoor bowls and darts.

Leaving the second tee at Lees Hall Golf Club in an exhibition match in May 1936, from left to right: Arthur Lees, Professional at Dore & Totley; Frank Jowle, Assistant Professional at Lees Hall, who achieved a record low score of 63 in the Open at St Andrew's New Course; Percy Allis, Ryder Cup player and father of Peter Allis, the well-known TV golf commentator (himself a Ryder Cup player); Leslie Powell, Professional at Lees Hall, holder of the record score of 60 for the course. Sadly, Mr Powell died in 1943, still a young man.

Above: In 1804 Cowmouth Farm was linked to Bolehill by a wide strip of common land. In the mid–1800s, Cowmouth was farmed by the Carr family, then by Mr Knowles, who eventually sold the business to Express Dairies. The old farm buildings and modern dairy on Hemsworth Road were then taken over by Associated Co-operative Creameries and, quite recently, by Dairy Farmers of Britain.

Left: Mr Thomas Lee worked for Sheffield Parks Department until he was seventy-six years old. His experience was greatly valued by the Head Keeper in Graves Park, especially during the war. He planted the floral displays and kept the rose garden in top condition, seen here in 1950. He also cared for St James's churchyard and prepared the Vicarage Field for May Day celebrations.

The Poplars in Bolehill, a Grade II-listed seventeenth-century house, was the home of the Linneker or Linacre family for about 200 years. John, Ravel and James were noted scythe and sickle makers. The name Bole Hill indicates an ancient lead smelting area, usually found on high ground, where wind could help produce a good fire in the furnace.

The Bole Hill hamlet still exists; several cottages date from the seventeenth century and traces of industry can be seen in the gardens. The parish registers list the occupations of scythe smith, scythe striker, scythe finisher, cutler and nail maker. The pump, which was on common ground for public use, is rather dilapidated now.

After enemy bombing damaged part of Norton Council School at Mundella Place in 1940, several 'House School' groups were formed. These children met at 251 Derbyshire Lane, home of the Hirst family. From left to right, back row: Keith Warrington, Alan Donohoe, Barry Smith. The front row includes Sheila Hicks and ? Jowell.

Opposite, above: Derbyshire Lane 'Feast' took place on a field opposite Mundella School, here possibly around 1910. Small fairs toured the country, providing simple entertainment. Swing boats can be seen behind the hut on the right, also a Galloping Horses roundabout. There is only one adult with these children; perhaps she is an anxious teacher in charge of all the juniors.

Opposite, below: The children of the Junior 4 class, Norton Council School, shortly before they finished at this school in July 1962. With them are Headmaster Mr Saunders and teacher Mr Morris. Do you recognise yourself or a friend?

The Prince Rovers football team's manager and trainer was Billy Claxton, of Harvey Clough Road. The name came from the Prince of Wales public house on Derbyshire Lane, where the team met occasionally to pay subscriptions and organise matches. The players in 1950 were, from left to right, back row: Eric Coulton, -?-, Tony Harrison, Dennis Paramore, George Beet, Keith Warrington. Front row: Rex Hollingsworth, Ken Claxton (son of the founder), Roy Palfreyman, Eric Draper, -?-.

Heeley Wesleyan Chapel Cricket XI with 'The Cup!' Some members had been called up for military service by 1916 but nevertheless a successful team was fielded. The young ladies, including sisters Florrie and Mary Dixon and their friend Mabel Bishop from Woodseats, supported the team and made the tea.

Above and below: For over 400 years Norton Lees Hall was home to wealthy yeomen and scythe makers, owners of waterwheels and property. The surname Parker is always associated with the Hall. The 1615 inventory of John Parker's goods illustrates a large house equipped with cotton, linen and silk furnishings, glass, pewter and silver, books and musical instruments. Wool, flax, farm animals and implements are also listed. Harry and Florence Earp and their son and daughter were the last family to rent Lees Hall. Mrs Earp used the rich milk from her goat to make ice cream and sold it to walkers.

Above: These are some of the remains of farm buildings at Lees Hall in 1958, after demolition had started. The stone walls and stone roof slates give an idea of the age of the farm. Between here and the site of Cockshutt Farm, walkers are intrigued by the many small pieces of mother-of-pearl on the path. Were buttons made locally?

Left: The lower side of Cockshutt Farm, situated above Lees Hall on the track up to Norton. The book *Chantreyland* includes a drawing of the white building, labelling it as a cottage. A very faded photograph of the uphill side shows a well-built stone farmhouse, steps to a storage loft, a small cart and haystacks. This peaceful place was demolished in 1958 and is now beneath the grounds of Newfield School.

five

A Leap in Time

John de Blythe received a grant of a messuage and land at the Lys in Norton in 1376. One line of the family remained at the Lees for hundreds of years, during which time the house was enlarged into its present form. It has been restored as the Bishops' House Museum, referring to John Blythe, Bishop of Salisbury, who died in 1499 and his brother Geoffrey, Bishop of Coventry and Lichfield, who died in 1531.

Samuel Blythe was the last of the family to live in the Bishops' House. He was a dissenting minister, given licence to hold services in his home. When he died in 1735, the property was sold to the Shore family. The stone cottages on the left, now demolished, housed employees of Mr Joseph Hall, who lived nearby at The Hollies, in the early 1900s.

Right: Mr Ryalls was a gardener who lived in one of the stone cottages to the east of the Bishops' House. A date of 1900 to 1910 has been suggested for this charming family group.

Below: Land for Meersbrook Park was acquired in 1886, then added to in 1928. These men, including Mr Ryalls, were able to keep warm on a snowy day!

Blythe

William Blythe, father of the bishops, obtained a grant of arms in 1485. In simple terms, the background bears the symbol for ermine, upon which is shown three red roe bucks with golden antlers. The crest is a roe buck's head, in the same colours, with a garland of green laurel about its neck. *In Veritate Victoria* translates as 'In Integrity is Victory'.

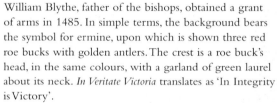

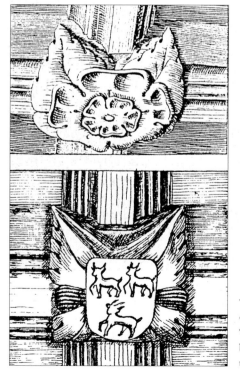

The chantry chapel of St Katherin, endowed by Bishop Geoffrey in memory of his parents, was built in 1524. The Tudor woodwork of the roof has splendid carved bosses, including the roe bucks of the coat-of-arms of the Blythe family and a Tudor rose.

One of only two photographs known of the interior of St James's Church before its restoration in 1881. Both photographs are cared for at Sheffield Archives as part of the Jackson Collection (ref. JC 1277 p.3d). This tomb of William and Saffery Blythe still exists but the wall with the 'pie-crust' top and the funeral hatchments above have been removed. The wall surrounded an area which was divided in 1718 to provide burial places for the families of Stephen Offley and Richard Bagshawe, the two main landowners in Norton.

Norton Woodseats and Norton Lees Parish Magazine.

DIVINE SERVICE.
Sunday Morning at 11.0.
Sunday Evening at 6.30.
Men's Service, Sunday Afternoon at 3.

HOLY COMMUNION.
1st and 3rd Sundays in the Month, Midday ; 4th Sunday in the Month, Evening ; 2nd and 5th Sundays, 8 a.m. in Summer ; 8.30 a.m. in Winter.

HOLY BAPTISM.
Sunday at 4.0 p.m.
Monday at 3.0 p.m.

ALL SEATS ARE FREE.

Notices of Banns and of Marriages should be given to the Clerk, Mr. Frank Farnsworth 56, Norton Lees Lane.

Clergy—Rev. V. ODOM, B.A., (Surrogate).
Rev W. A. BIRKS, B.A.
Churchwardens—Mr. W. PITCHFORD, Mr. T. LEECH.
Organist—Mr. W. A. BLAKELEY.
Choirmaster—Mr. WALTER LUDGATE.

SUNDAY SCHOOLS.
WOODSEATS: Cammell's School, 10 a.m. ; 2.30 p.m.
DERBYSHIRE LANE : Club House, 10.30 a.m. ; 2.30 p.m.
NORTON LEES : PARISH HALL, 2.30 p.m,
YOUNG WOMEN'S BIBLE CLASS : Church Vestry, 3.15 p.m

MEETINGS.
MISSION SERVICES : Cammell's Schoolroom, } Sunday and Club House, Derbyshire Lane, } 6.30 p.m.
MOTHERS' MEETING : Club House, Monday, 2.15 p.m.
YORKSHIRE PENNY BANK : Club House, Saturday, 7 p.m.

The Vicar requests that he may be informed of cases of illness where a visit from him would be welcome.

W. W. Askew Printer, Norfolk Printing Works, 51, Norfolk Street Sheffield.

Norton Woodseats and Norton Lees Parish Magazine from March 1911, costing 1d.

St Paul's Church members worked hard to raise funds for their Parish Hall and Institute, which opened in 1909, but were still in debt in 1911. These ladies continued to sell cakes, aprons and other handwork. They embroidered their signatures on a tablecloth and this was placed under glass on a table in the Hall as a reminder of their efforts.

Norton Lees Ladies' Sewing Party.
Mar. 8—Mrs. Atkinson, 63, Woodbank Crescent
 ,, 15—Mrs. Lister, 40, Crescent Road.
 ,, 22—Mrs. Pitchford, 82, Burcot Road.
 ,, 29—Mrs. Fletcher, 35, Brook Road.

The Woodseats Ladies' Sewing Party meets over Mr. Washington's shop, 772, Chesterfield Road, on Wednesday afternoons from 3 to 7. Tea, sixpence each, provided by
Mar. 1—Mrs. C. Morton.
 ,, 8—Mrs. Hunstone.
 ,, 15—Mrs. Feltrup.
 ,, 22—Mrs. H. Sampson.
 ,, 30—(Thursday) Mrs. Hallworth, at 14, Linburn Road.

In the parish magazine of 11 March 1911 is a drawing of a proposed new church to be built in Linden Avenue. The square bell-tower shown here was never built. The foundation stone of St Chad's was laid by Mrs B.A. Firth of Norton Hall in August 1911. The first vicar was the Revd G. Cuthbert Kydd.

Left: George Constantine was born in 1869 and lived in Norton Lees. He sang in the choir at St James's Church and is remembered as the choirmaster in the 1930s. His son was also in the choir and took part in concert parties, plays and musical shows in Norton and Woodseats.

Below: E.A. Constantine sketched the four cottages below St Paul's Church, at right angles to Norton Lees Lane. Two were knocked down to make a turning place for buses when they came out to Norton Lees in 1926 and the other two were demolished in 1962. The whole site became Norton Lees Garage. The Marshall girls lived in the top cottage and remember seeing coloured lights shining through the stained-glass windows of St Paul's Church and on to their bedroom wall.

Another view of the row of cottages on Norton Lees Lane, plus part of the only other cottage on that side of the lane near the church. The Thompson family lived there for many years before it, too, was knocked down in the 1930s.

The shop of E. & E. Bell stood at the corner of Derbyshire Lane and Scarsdale Road. Many memories will be stirred by the advertisements for tea, cigarettes and holidays in 'Skeggy' and by the red telephone box. Mr Bell's car is parked in the yard. A small length of dropped pavement edge, once the yard entrance, is the only remaining trace of these shops.

Prices of groceries in 1911 offer 'food' for thought. To help younger readers, 1/4 means one shilling and four pence. The boot polish on offer cost one modern penny. Does anyone recall cocoa essence?

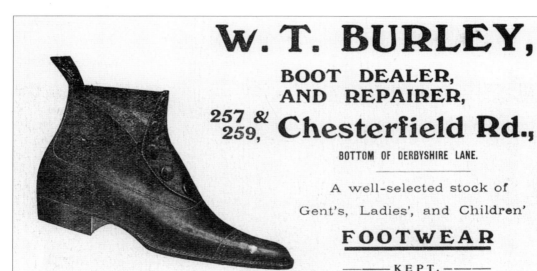

Styles seem to come round in a fashion circle and the boot in this 1911 advertisement looks fairly modern. It is hard to imagine any cobbler nowadays collecting shoes for repair on receipt of a postcard!

In the nineteenth century, Samuel Gillatt and his family were cattle dealers and farmers of land stretching from Norton Lees down the hill to the present Dale and Woodseats area. It is not surprising that Ivy Farm, situated at the junction of the Dale and Woodseats Road, was more commonly known then as Gillatt's Farm. Samuel Gillatt was an active member of St James's Church, where his family memorial can be seen on the north aisle wall.

Alderman J.G. Graves presented The Graves Shield for netball in 1927. The first finalists were Woodseats Council School girls and the runners-up were Anns Road Council School girls.

727, CHESTERFIELD ROAD, WOODSEATS,

(HALLAMSHIRE BANK BUILDINGS,)

Sheffield, *Mar 16* 1912

M

Bought of MRS. POWELL.

Ladies Outfitter.

3	Vests	11½	2	10½	
1	Head Square		2	6	
2	Barras	1/4½	2	9	
1	"		2	6	
1	Skirt		2	6	
1	Robe		4	11	
2	Cream Gowns	1/10½	3	11	
2	Gowns	1/11½	3	11	
1	"		1	4½	
			1 7 3½		
2	Binders 5½		11		
½	7d Flannel 1/3½		8		
	Pins 6½ Puff 4½ Thread		1 0		
			1 9 10		

Paid with Thanks
G. W. Powell
mar 16/1912

Mrs Powell's shop, selling goods for ladies and babies, was situated in the Hallamshire Bank Buildings, now HSBC, at Woodseats. Binders and half a yard of flannel, together with the other items listed on the receipt, perhaps suggest shopping for a newly born baby.

Mrs Clarissa Bower outside the family's hardware shop at the bottom of Olivet Road, near the Woodseats Hotel, in 1912. The packed window display includes broom heads, hand brushes, shopping bags, pans, kettles and egg-cups. The small funnels, or tun-dishes, were used to fill lamps with paraffin; Mr Bower delivered paraffin into Derbyshire. The shop was also a receiving office for the Ruskin Laundry and hired out bicycles.

Above: Holmhirst Road Methodist Church was finished in 1916, the only church in the UK to be allowed to finish its construction during the First World War. This view of the interior was taken in 2001 to show the layout of the church before the removal of the pulpit and adjacent woodwork.

Left: Mr Walter Williams moved to Woodseats in 1905 and founded his bicycle business shortly afterwards. The original shop on the corner of Helmton Road and Chesterfield Road has been added to and now, two generations on, Williams of Woodseats is an excellent supplier of electrical goods. Mr Williams contributed to the life of Woodseats; for many years he was the choirmaster at Chantrey Road Methodist Church.

Vale Cottage was more or less where Woodseats Library is today. There was an apple orchard at the back and a small field between the house and the road. Some people can recall the Gyte family who lived here in the 1930s, when Mr Gyte's main business was as a motor haulage contractor.

Another peaceful farmhouse, just above the Gyte's, where Mr Arthur Anderson lived in the 1930s. He was a milk dealer and it is probably his milk cart at the front of the barn. The field was purchased for road-widening and Jack Marshall's garage, more recently Peter Brooks Honda dealership, was built on the site of the house by Bromwich Road.

The Whit Monday Walks were a reminder of Christian Witness in the area. Processions from local churches would make their way through the streets, often with banners and bands, to an ecumenical service in Graves Park. Members of the Woodseats Methodist Churches in 1953 include John and Harry Parsons, Dorothy Sizer, Michael Longden and Mrs Coe.

The Meadowhead Lodge was the largest of the lodges on the three approach drives to Norton Hall but was demolished to make way for new housing. The lodge end of the drive became the present Charles Ashmore Road while the far end was reduced to a path, following the route of the drive through Graves Park to Norton Hall.

Rowland Unwin, the nephew of Ernest Hunstone of Park Farm, sitting on the pump at Little Norton Green in 1934. The Green was common land between Park Farm orchard, seen in the background, and the cottages and pig farm nearby.

The first modern house to be occupied in 1935 on Little Norton Lane was No. 75. Mr Herbert Fruer Bridges, his wife Ethel and Miss Nellie Godwin found that gardening was hard work. They had to dig up the foundations of huts which were part of the No. 1 Camp for men in the First World War. Soldiers working at the No. 2 (Northern) Aircraft Repair Depot lived in this camp.

The Haig Memorial Homes, Ogden Place, Meadowhead were built in 1929 for severely wounded ex-servicemen. Most of them were Sheffield men but others, including a Canadian, came from farther away. They were employed at the nearby Painted Fabrics Ltd workshops.

David Carter, great-nephew of Annie Bindon Carter, unveiled this memorial plaque in August 2000. The hand-painted fabrics produced at Little Norton were of such a high quality that they were sold in major London stores and exported throughout the world.

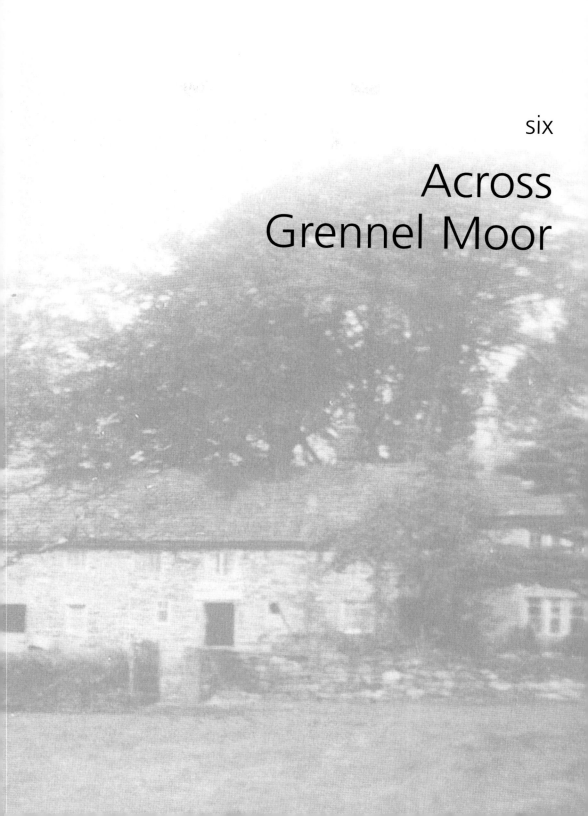

six

Across
Grennel Moor

The 1902 Coronation Celebration Dinner at the White Swan, Greenhill. In the background are the cottages and forge at the junction of School Lane and Annesley Road. A fine display of turn-of-the-century fashion!

Opposite, above and below: The row of four houses on the left in the top picture can still be seen in Greenhill Main Road. Mr Apthorpe kept the post office here in the 1930s. Later, Nos 51 and 55 became The Fruit and Flower Bowl greengrocery and The Cutting Edge hairdressing shops. Coming back along Main Road, Miss Elms's confectionery shop was in the cottage on the far right. The house fronting onto the bend, remembered as Mr Dalton's newsagency, faced the old cottages and the public pump in the lower picture. The pump has been retained as part of the history of Greenhill and in recent years has been the site of a well dressing.

This top corner of Bocking Lane, *c.* 1970, shows plenty of activity centred on the row of shops. The grocery shops, chemist, baker and post office were well used by young mothers, judging by the range of pram styles and the red telephone box was handy for the many people who did not have a 'phone at home. The road sign appears to have dropped down the pole and been turned through ninety degrees!

The businesses above have gone but the area still has a wide range of shops reflecting changing lifestyles.

A roundabout now occupies Greenhill Hollow. Bocking Lane leads off to the left and Greenhill Main Road runs uphill by the former fields where Greenhill School now stands. These cottages, marked on a 1906 map, gave way to shops of the Sheffield & Ecclesall Co-operative Society. By the 1920s, an outdoor aerial of the type seen here was a standard requirement for an early wireless radio receiver.

This hut, in the grounds of the old Greenhill School, was demolished in 2001. In the 1940s there was a classroom at each end and visiting medical staff used small rooms in the centre. A doctor weighed, measured and gave a general health inspection to the children, a nit-nurse combed their hair and a dentist checked their teeth.

Weekly sewing class in the garden of the Misses Seymour in Meadowhead Avenue in 1951, making items for sale at the church fêtes held in Greenhill School. Girls with Miss Seymour include Eleanor Drewery, Margaret Simpson, Margaret Sowerby, Ann Sowerby, Catherine Drewery, Cynthia Thornhill, Christine Robinson, Pat Gomersall and Susan Chalmers.

St Peter's Greenhill church choir in 1957, at the altar end of the temporary church building. From left to right, back row: –?–, Margaret Simpson, Diane Currie, Christine Currie, Terry Pearson, Vivienne Wanty, Mrs Olle, Miss Seymour. Middle row: John Walter Simpson (PCC secretary), Henry Wilson (organist and choirmaster), Mr Godwin (church warden), the Revd R.D.G. Owen, Mr Newton (church warden and PCC treasurer), Mr Johnson. Front row: Peter Startup, –?–, John Simpson, –?–, Alan Hever, the Millington twins, Derek and Stuart, –?–.

Summer garden party at Bradway in 1955, with all three Church May Queens in attendance, Judith Reed (Norton), Vivienne Wanty (Bradway) and Margaret Simpson (Greenhill). Others enjoying the day include Frances Beckett, the Revd Owen, Kathleen Higginson, Wendy ?, Christine Robinson, Ann Truelove, Councillor Tindall and Mrs May Owen.

Handbell ringers at the first May Queen ceremony in the combined church and church hall in Reney Avenue, Greenhill, opened in 1954. This building was not needed when St Peter's was built in 1964 and The Avenue Medical Centre is now on the site. From left to right: Christine Sutton, Sheila Dickinson, Keith Millington, Michael Hague, Tony Jury, Neville Sheldon.

A fifth-year form in 1980-1981 at Jordanthorpe School, by then a mixed Comprehensive school. From left to right, back row: Patrick Stonehewer, Dominic Lee, John Thorpe, Neil Odell, Dominic Swift, Ian Glaves, Glenn Jacques, Andrew Vinson, Richard Astle. Middle row: Greg Thompson, Catherine Scott, Jill Copley, Andrea Pennington, Alison Oldman, Debbie Skelton, Jane Oldfield, Julie Evans, Mandy Stark, Janet Barker, Neil Frost. Front row: Ruth Spiers, Tim Kemplay, Frances Bower, Catherine Lawrence, Jenny Bowker (form teacher), Alison Corley, Jonathan Greatorex, Brian Jackson, Andrew Coldwell.

Opposite, above: The very busy Meadowhead roundabout was a crossroads controlled by traffic lights until major road works in the area in the 1970s. On the far right is Jordanthorpe Boys' School, which was opened in September 1954 as a Secondary Modern School.

Opposite, below: A small wind and brass group at Jordanthorpe Boys' Secondary School. Their teacher, Jim Kirkwood, did much to produce good music and singing at the school. Later, he was asked to conduct the Radio Sheffield choir in Christmas concerts at the City Hall.

JUBILEE
AIR DISPLAYS

VALID FOR ONE FLIGHT ONLY

MONGOOSE

1935

CHILD 2/6 CHILD

PER PASSENGER.

Issued by Jubilee Air Displays Ltd.,
101, Leadenhall Street, London, E.C.3.
Subject to Conditions Printed Overleaf.
TO BE RETAINED BY PASSENGER.

Left: Written above this ticket: 'My first flight, at the age of 13 in 1935, was in an AVRO 506N with a Mongoose engine, piloted by Des Howarth. I won this flight guessing the height at 9,750 ft.' The Jubilee referred to was the Silver Jubilee of the accession of King George V.

Below: The Admiralty occupied buildings off Norton Lane during the Second World War, on land which is now beneath the grounds of the Norton campus, Sheffield College. The work was very 'hush-hush' and the entrance gates were well guarded in 1944 by Mr Ludlam and his colleague of the Admiralty Civil Police.

A glimpse of Princess Margaret being driven along Dyche Lane after opening Rowlinson Technical School on a Saturday in 1953. The princess was dressed in black, still in mourning for Queen Mary. The lane was lined with onlookers, some reflected in the windows of the car.

Rowlinson Comprehensive School football team in 1976, lined up on the hard playing area, with Norton Lane houses in the background. From left to right, back row: David Stennel, Paul Redman, Richard Andrews, Mark Jarvis, Steven Loxley, Brendan Griffith. Front row: John Ellis, Craig Shackleton, Steven Brammer, David Gibson, John Brakes.

Mr Frank V. Shepherd became the farmer at Jordanthorpe Farm in 1934 when yet another piece of Derbyshire was bought by Sheffield Corporation. The barns and yard were close to Jordanthorpe House, in the area where Mossbrook School stands today.

The dairy at Jordanthorpe Farm in 1944, showing a cooler, buckets, milk churn and bottles. Later, milk was sent to the dairy on Hemsworth Road for bottling and distribution.

The football team of No. 248 Prisoner-of-War Camp with David Shepherd, son of Frank Shepherd of Jordanthorpe Farm, in 1946. In this post-war period the men were free to move about in the village from their camp at the farm. One German, Paul Weisser, wrote to his local newspaper in 1992, recalling the 1946 Christmas Eve service at St James's.

George Shepherd feeding wire into the baler, Don Culf and Richard Shepherd pitching, Mr Shepherd on the tractor and Angela Finnegan on the rake. The rake was pulled by one of Mr Shepherd's fine horses. Another horse, named Winston, had a day of glory as part of the team pulling the Lord Mayor of London's coach.

Austin Revitt harrowing a Jordanthorpe Farm field off Dyche Lane in the spring of 1941. The background is of great interest because the wartime Civil Service buildings can be seen on the left. These seem to be the ones used by the Fire Service in later years.

Mr Austin Revitt, a champion ploughman, here being presented with a Ploughing Cup by Mrs Muriel Isherwood-Bagshawe. Miss Gladys Bagshawe is on the left and we hope to be told the names of the other onlookers.

Mr Parkes, a ploughman for Mr Peat of Cross Lane, off Dyche Lane, ready to show his skills during the 1995 Ploughing Match. What a difference from the machinery used fifty years earlier.

The very hot summer of 1976 brought danger to local farms. Stubble burning was allowed at that time and many fires broke out in fields and stack yards throughout the country. The local fire station had moved to Low Edges, still near enough to respond quickly.

The ancient cruck building of Jordanthorpe Hall Farm, taken by no less a photographer than Mrs Isherwood-Bagshawe herself, c.1935. The farm and barn have been modified in recent years to form two houses, now in a rather less peaceful setting beside the busy bypass.

During the construction of the Bochum Parkway, which opened on 28 June 1982, this ancient cruck barn, at the lower side of the yard at Jordanthorpe Hall Farm, was demolished. Luckily it was photographed and recorded by the County Archaeologist, Peter Ryder, and by a local historian, Mrs Bunker.

Above: Some of John Bullifant's family and his horses in the field at the far end of Cinderhill Lane, known as Far Field.

Right: Emily Bullifant, her brother Douglas and dog outside the front door of Jordanthorpe Hall Farm, *c.* 1932.

The rear elevation of the eighteenth-century Chantry Cottage showed interesting details of the central staircase windows. The back and ends of the cottage have been altered considerably in recent years.

Some of the cold frames and greenhouses in the Sheffield Recreation Department Nursery at Norton Lane in 1990, by which time they were not in use any more. Thousands of plants were grown here and then planted throughout the city, giving Sheffield a country-wide reputation for top-quality floral displays.

seven

Times
Remembered

Left and below: Well dressings were a feature on the Green during the Norton Weeks held each June in the 1970s and 1980s. The heavy boards of the framework were soaked in the Oakes lake for some time, then brought to the Youth Hall where kneaded clay was keyed in among wooden pegs to make a solid, moisture-holding base. Teams of volunteers worked for about two weeks, marking out the design with pins and wool and inserting the petals with a knitting needle. Many local gardens were raided for flowers and Norton Nursery often came to the rescue, particularly with blue hydrangea petals for sky and water.

Right: Private Arthur Shaw of the Highland Light Infantry was born at Mawfa Lane in 1884. He was appointed as the first professional at Norton Lees Golf Club in 1908, receiving payment of one shilling per hour. He fought in the First World War, dying in hospital in January 1918. His name is on the Norton War Memorial and his grave, in Norton Cemetery, is in the care of the Commonwealth War Graves Commission.

Below: The additional stone on the War Memorial was dedicated on Remembrance Sunday in November 1999 by the Rector of St James's, the Revd M. Morgan. The stone is polished granite and was made by G. Paramore & Sons, masons of Abbey Lane.

JOSEPH L. RAWLINS,
PROFESSOR OF MUSIC,
ORGANIST AND CHOIRMASTER OF NORTON PARISH CHURCH.

B EGS to inform his Friends and the Public, that he gives Lessons on the
ORGAN,

PIANOFORTE,

HARMONIUM, &c.,

TERMS : One Pupil £1 1s., for Eleven Lessons : Two or more members of one family 18/- each.

The QUARTER commences FROM the Date of the FIRST LESSON. Pupils visited (on Wednesdays) in Dronfield and the neighbourhood. TUNING.—Terms for Dronfield and district 4s.

Address—Cliffe Feld Terrace, Meersbrook Bank, Sheffield.

Dronfield Parish Magazine of April 1884 contained an advertisement from the organist and choirmaster of St James's Church, Professor Rawlins. He was a member of the West Yorkshire Yeomanry Cavalry Band in 1880, when he lived at Hope Cottage, Norton Woodseats.

St James's has had a male choir for more than a century, new boys being recruited from local primary schools. From left to right, back row: Richard Robinson, Harry Jow, Mr Barden, Bernard ?, -?-, Fred Rodgers, Norman Jones, Harry Coombs, Malcolm Smith. Middle row: -?-, -?-, Andy Smith, Alan Vardy, choir master John Allen, the Revd Canon Gledhill, Geoff Vardy, -?-, Richard Shepherd, -?-. Front row: John Humphrey, David Marshall, Paul Wood, -?-.

Did the members of the Norton Church Choir and Junior Bible Class who joined their newly formed football club manage to keep to the rules? The subscription was one shilling and sixpence, one shilling to be paid before the first match and the balance at the end of the first month. The first captain was W.H. Mawkes and the vice-captain was A. Coupe.

That the Ground for Practice be in the Oakes Park and no other —

That any Member using bad Language be fined 1d and after a second offence be liable to be expelled at the discretion of the Committee —

That the Committee meet in the Vicarage Room on Tuesday evenings at 8 o'clock

That five form a Quorum

The Norton Church Choir Football Team in 1947 turned out in their strip of dark blue body and light blue collar and sleeves. From left to right, back row: Keith Bentley, Peter Lee, Eric Powell, Gerald Hall, -?-, John Talford, Tony Jowle. Front row: Tony Knott, Frank Milner, Malcolm Stobbs, Alan Hodkinson, Michael Hodinott.

Norton Church Reading Rooms

...IN...

The CHURCH COTTAGE, GREENHILL,

The BRADWAY MISSION ROOM,

The CHURCH COTTAGE, BACKMOOR,

The VICARAGE ROOM

→≡•OPEN•≡←

MONDAYS, WEDNESDAYS & SATURDAYS,

7-30 P.M. until 9-30 P.M.

Admit

Signed,
G. W. HALL, Vicar.

RULES.

1.—No admission without Ticket.

2.—No smoking allowed.

3.—No bad language.

4.—No gambling.

5.—No rough behaviour.

6.—No books, papers or games to be taken TO, or removed FROM, the Room.

7.—Any member infringing the above rules will be debarred from further use of the Reading Room.

Above and left: The Hemsworth Reading Room was in the courthouse between 1887 and 1888 and then in the Church Cottage, Backmoor, until 1893. The Reading and Recreation Room for Young Men in Greenhill was in the Church Cottage before 1887, after which one of the schoolrooms was used.

Opposite, below: The St James's Sunday school May Queen in 1972, standing outside the Youth Hall, was Helen Ackroyd. The School Captain was Nigel Rothwell and the crown-bearer was David Bland. The attendants were, from left to right: Beverley Pulford, Lorraine Dewar, -?- and -?-.

The joint Bradway, Greenhill and Norton Sunday schools held an annual treat, usually consisting of games and a party tea. This group gathered in the yard at Norton Rectory in the late 1940s.

Above: Norton Free School children often participated in summertime church events. A good crowd is watching the school team of maypole dancers on the Green in 1982.

Right: Older people still remember Bertrand Shaw and his wife, who gave many hours of service to St James's Church. They lived in Maugerhay and Mr and Mrs Vardy remember walking down the track to the cottage to confirm the date of their wedding in 1940. Many people have mentioned Bert fetching his stepladder during a service to attend to a smoking paraffin lamp.

John (Jack) Moreton Vardy and his bride Margaret *née* Thompson outside St James's Church after their wartime wedding on 30 March 1940.

Jack Vardy and his daughter Sylvia were greeted by Canon Gledhill and members of St James's Church choir and escorted to the church for her wedding to Martin Tongue on 2 August 1969. Her two brothers were in the church, Alan as best man and Geoffrey as part of the team providing the welcoming peal of bells.

The Chantrey Club, organized by Ruby Randall, met in the Church Hall each week but occasionally were invited to Norton Hall. This group on the front steps at Norton Hall in 1973 includes, at the back, Mrs Wilson, Mrs Lees and Mrs Stella Nelmes and at the front, Mrs Constance Bacon, Mrs Winnie Leesley and Mrs Peggy Rowley.

32nd Sheffield Company Mount View Boys' Brigade band at the Jessop Hospital annexe, Norton Hall, on Whit Sunday 1947. Standing, from left to right: Company Captain Ted James, John Smith, Eric Parkin, Jack Lancaster, Peter Thorpe, Peter Draper, Joe Winter, Malcolm Burrell, Alan Johnson, Maurice Swift, Raymond Brown, Alan Sharpe, Terry Woodward, -?-, and second in command Eric Broadhead. Kneeling: Brian Millington, Trevor Thompson, Gordon Wilkinson, Ken Claxton, Keith Warrington, Revill May.

The Girl Guides of the 48th St James's Company helping at a garden party at Norton Rectory in the early 1950s are, from left to right: Susan Priestley, Mollie Wilson, Julia Hole and Margaret Bolsover.

The 280th St James's Norton Scout Troop was started in 1915. These boys, including Nicky Robinson at the far left and Andy Gilmour at the far right, were at a 1969 Jamboree at St David's in Wales. The Chief Scout, Sir Charles MacLean, had perfected a bone-crushing Scout handshake!

Christianity spread to Norton through the preaching of the monk later known as Saint Chad. The play *Chad* was written by the curate of St James's, the Revd Simon Bailey, as an interpretation of Chad's work. It was performed in the churchyard at Norton in July 1985 and was a community effort involving many local organisations, including these children from Norton Free School.

Other local schools took part, including Dr John Bingham and Hemsworth. These children from Hazlebarrow School acted as monks and are here taking a break from rehearsal.

The principal actors in *Chad*, standing, left to right: Richard Proctor, Stuart Bamber, Heather Gatley, the Revd Mollie Kenyon, the Revd Simon Bailey, Margaret Turley, Richard Bland, Caroline Brown. Front row: Matthew Tongue, Caroline Snape, Mark Simpson.

A scene during the performance of *Chad*. The play was presented each day during Norton Week in 1985.

Left and below: A joint production by St Chad's and St James's Dramatic Societies of a pageant representing the life of St Thomas à Becket was performed at Beauchief Abbey in 1970. These photographs, taken during rehearsals, include Bert Lowe as FitzRanulph, Ruby Randall, Vera Rathbone, Bill Rawson as FitzUrse, Cecil Ridgeway, Connie Rodgers and Eric Smith as de Moreville. Other principal actors were Len Bradwell as Becket and Ian Kemlo as King Henry II.

Another community effort on 2 July 1983 was a pageant depicting a thousand years of life in Norton. The parade assembled in the grounds of the Oakes. The Link-16 youth group depicting St Thomas à Becket were, from left to right, back row: Kieran Hush, Alison Phipps, Alison Townsley, Jo Williams, Christina Wells, Carl Bamber, Anna Heap, Steven Proctor. Front row: Matthew Barnett, Andrew Phipps, Caroline Brown, Adam Simpson, Adrian Wells.

St James's Guides represented Saxon times and included, from left to right, back row: Lorraine Stirland, Assistant Guider Jean Horton, Guider Anne Phipps. Front row: Claire Bamber, Paula Hird, Amanda ?, Helen Ward, Nicola Barker, Jane Kenyon.

Local firms lent their lorries as floats, this one used by the Pam Torrey School of Dance pupils, who met in the Church Hall. They include Mrs Sue Gilbody, Helena Brough, Louise Hayley, Rachel Greenwood, Joanne Waters, Natalie Kay, Caroline Frith and Angela Booth.

This float depicts the story of Robert Raikes, the founder of the Sunday School Movement. St James's Sunday school members include Mrs Liz Parkes, Helen Vardy, Elizabeth Vardy, Ron Parkes, Rachel Musgrave Gemma Booth and Mrs Glen Musgrave.

The 147th St James's Jordanthorpe Brownies represented early flight in Norton. Four dads, Michael Shelton, Alan Watkinson, John Watkinson and Jim Whelan, made the aircraft from strong cardboard. The girls made their own helmets, cleverly using egg boxes for their goggles.

After the parade there was a Victorian fair in the churchyard and a sheep roast on the Green by the Chantrey Monument, followed by an Elizabethan banquet in Norton Hall. The Pre-School Playgroup Association stall was run by Sue Smith, Sue Rogers and Conchi Hooton. Their eager customer is Matthew Jarvis.

Other local titles published by Tempus

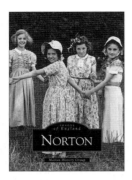

Norton
NORTON HISTORY GROUP

This fascinating collection of over 200 old photographs records the vanished rural community of Norton as it was in the early twentieth century. The parish was encroached upon by the city of Sheffield in several stages after 1900, and this expansion changed the nature of the area forever. The book is divided into thematic chapters dealing with different aspects of life, including schooldays, churches, home life and local services, and is sure to appeal to all those who know Norton.

0 7524 2052 6

Sheffield Parks and Gardens
DOUGLAS HINDMARCH

Sheffield is justifiably proud of the parks, woodlands and open spaces which make it one of the greenest cities in Europe. However, in the early nineteenth century the town was overcrowded and polluted and there were no green spaces for leisure and recreation. This book illustrates how the parks and gardens were acquired and developed from the 1830s onwards, and shows some of the park features which have now disappeared. Also depicted are everyday events and special occasions such as Whitsuntide gatherings and royal visits.

0 7524 3542 6

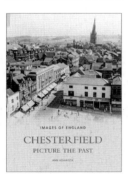

Chesterfield: Picture the Past
ANN KRAWSZIK

This collection of over 200 old photographs of Chesterfield is a sample of the many thousands of images which are now available to view on the award-winning website www.picturethepast.org.uk. These images, many never before published, provide a fascinating pictorial history of Chesterfield over the past 150 years. The result is a book that will delight anyone who has lived or worked in this beautiful town.

0 7524 3581 7

Sheffield Cinemas
CLIFFORD SHAW FOR THE SHEFFIELD CINEMA SOCIETY

The first purpose-built cinema in Sheffield was the Picture Palace in Union Street, which opened in 1910. By the outbreak of war in 1914, there were thirty cinemas either completed or under construction. Cinemas suffered a slump during the 1920s but were revived by the advent of the 'talkies' in 1929/30. This pictorial compilation places on record some of the history of local cinemas; it is a reminder of what once was.

0 7524 2293 6

If you are interested in purchasing other books published by Tempus, or in case you have difficulty finding any Tempus books in your local bookshop, you can also place orders directly through our website

www.tempus-publishing.com